MAGICAL SENSE

BY MALCOLM DE CHAZAL

TRANSLATED BY JEAN BONNIN

Also by Jean Bonnin

Novels:

A Certain Experience of the Impossible (2009)

Lines Within The Circle (2012)

The Cubist's House (2015)

One Eyed Fish (2016)

Poetry and Articles:

Un-usual Muse-uals (2012)

Being and Somethingness (2015)

Translations:

Magical Science by Malcolm de Chazal (2016)

Jean Bonnin

Jean Bonnin was born in Lavaur, in the Tarn in France;
he was brought up mainly in the United Kingdom. He took his first
degree in government and politics at Birmingham, and his second
in political philosophy at Hull; his doctoral research was
on the theories of despotism. After university he lived and
worked in France, Portugal, Ireland, and the former
East Germany. On deciding to leave the underground and
avant-garde music scenes of Berlin and northern France behind
him – but not to abandon his music-making altogether –
he returned to Wales where he now lives and writes in his
empty house… empty, save for the Malcolm de Chazal
painting above his fireplace.

Magical Sense
An Original Publication of Red Egg Publishing
An imprint of Red Egg International
First published in the UK by Red Egg Publishing
in 2015
www.redeggpublishing.com

Copyright © Jean Bonnin 2015

Jean Bonnin has asserted his moral right to be identified as the sole author of this book (in its translated form, as it appears here).

Cover design: J. Bonnin

British Library Cataloguing-in-Publication Data
A catalogue record for this book is available upon request from the British Library

ISBN: 978-0-9571258-6-5

While every effort has been made to contact copyright-holders, if an acknowledgement has been overlooked, please contact the publisher

This book is sold subject to the condition that it shall not, by way of trade or otherwise, be lent, re-sold, hired out, or otherwise circulated without the publisher's prior consent in any form of binding or cover other than that in which it is published and without a similar condition including this condition being imposed on the subsequent purchaser

MAGICAL SENSE

BY MALCOLM DE CHAZAL

TRANSLATED BY JEAN BONNIN

INTRODUCTION

In 2009 my first novel was published. At around this time I was co-proprietor of a shop. It was a shop which, along with other curios, sold my first book and over the course of the next couple of years had my subsequent two other books for sale.

A woman who lived locally, called Yvelaine, who I didn't really know at the time, over a period of several months, purchased all three of my books. As time passed we gradually began to converse; either in the street, if our paths happened to cross, or on the instances when she bought one of my books. And thus it was soon established that she as I had a mixed French/British heritage and we also both had an interest in similar kinds of art and literature.

It was after one such chance meeting in approximately 2011 that eventually led to my becoming a devotee of this remarkable man Malcolm de Chazal…

Malcolm de Chazal

Malcolm de Chazal (1902-1981) – was born in Mauritius to French parents… To begin with he was a writer and a poet. Two of his most notable books being: *Sens Plastique* and *Sens Magique*… W.H. Auden said of him that he was "…the most original and interesting French writer to emerge since the war." And André Breton hailed him as a surrealist.

In 1950, at the suggestion of Georges Braque, he began to paint... Better known in the French-speaking world – as an influential artist who stands alone in both his approach and his style – he is now becoming appreciated in the English-speaking world as a free-thinker who is deserving of his place in art history.

He was seen as a surrealist, a mystic and an alchemist... Occasionally one glimpses similarities between his work and Van Gogh's, Matisse's and Derain's. He has been described as an abstract-surrealist expressionist. But, to my mind, he could be defined as a post-Fauvist. And if that *is* what he was, then he was the essence of what that approach was supposed to embody in its purest form: an animalistic and feral interpretation of the world through bold colours, harnessing the emotions whilst rejecting a rigid representational approach to art and the world.

Ultimately, and this is what is exciting about de Chazal, he is unlike any other artist… and as an extension, any other writer.

Not that that was exactly what Yvelaine told me. What she said was that she was looking for someone to translate one of de Chazal's most important works: *Sens Magique*. And that having read my style of writing thought I would be the ideal candidate. And this, then, more or less, was the story she recounted to me:

Malcolm de Chazal was born in Mauritius to French parents. And Yvelaine Armstrong was brought up for the first few years of her life on the island of Mauritius.

Yvelaine's mother Marie-France, who was an artist and poet in her own right, moved to the island during the sixties. A time when the independence movement from the British Empire was in full swing and when politically everything was in flux.

She loved de Chazal's work and soon became a very good friend of his. To the extent that it was she who procured many paints and paper for his pictures, persuading him to use better quality products than he had been.

Eventually, due to the closeness of their relationship, de Chazal fell in love with Yvelaine's mother and proposed marriage. Marie-France told him, however, that she didn't see him in that manner and just wished to remain good friends.

Then the time came when Marie-France was planning to return to London. Naturally, on hearing this news, he was upset, but at the same time he was excited. Excited by the possibilities this might present. He immediately brought her many of his paintings – all that were in his possession at the time. He did this in part as tokens of his gratitude and as a representation of the fondness he felt for her, but also as examples of his work for her to show galleries (which Marie-France did for many years afterwards). De Chazal instructed Marie-France to burn any that she considered to be of an inferior standard. Yvelaine indeed remembers seeing as a child the pile of paintings he'd brought around.

This amounted to hundreds of paintings, of course none of which she burnt. And now they constitute what is known as the *Armstrong Collection* – which, as far as anyone knows, was the largest single collection of Malcolm de Chazal's work.

Needless to say I accepted Yvelaine's offer and have spent the last three or four years either translating or thinking about translating the aphorisms, poems and philosophies to be found in Monsieur de Chazal's *Sens Magique*. Of course it didn't take me all of that time to translate his work (I naturally had my own writing that I was getting on with in the meantime), but in one sense or another I have lived with his words and his mind for all of that time…

This, then, is *Sense Magique*; Magical Wisdom, Magical Meanings… Magical Sense.

Jean Bonnin
Pembrokeshire
Wales, UK.
November 2015

MAGICAL SENSE

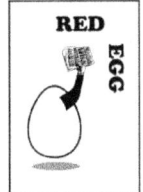

BY MALCOLM DE CHAZAL

TRANSLATED BY JEAN BONNIN

1.

A bicycle bowled
Along the road
The road
Is the third wheel
Which drives the other two.

2.

Water said to the wave
"You are drinking me."
"How could I do that?"
Replied the wave
"I am your mouth."

3.

The aeroplane travelled so quickly
The sun came to a standstill
The man in the cockpit
Was Joshua.

4.

The rose asked the sun
"Can you see me?"
"No," said the sun
"I am your eyes."

5.

When the fire
Licked up the wood
It saw that it licked its own hands:
Some sparks were in front of it.

6.

Two mountains
Were touching the cloud
With their peaks.
For an instant
The cloud believed
It was upside down
And searched in vain for its head.

7.

When the rain stopped weeping
I saw the dew laugh.
The sun was making fun of them.

8.

When the creeper
Grasped the branch
The branch gave way
And the flower turned its head
To see what was happening.

9.

When the dog
Hit his paw
Against the wall
He thought he had lost his leg.
He jumped sideways
And the wall leaned towards him.
Panic-stricken
The animal tucked its paws
Under its neck.

10.

The miser
Counted
His money so often
It appeared as though
He was counting golden fingers.

11.

"I have a cold"
Said grey
A red handkerchief
Appeared in front of him
And grey sneezed.

12.

The trees are climbing
This hillside.
Make a sheep climb up the hillside
And the trees would stop
In bewilderment.

13.

You feel worn out
You're wrong.
The wind feels warn out
That's why
You are no longer warm.

14.

The horse is on a short rein
He may win
As the reins
Pull him along.

15.

This jockey
Was so handicapped
By red
He would have won
If he'd worn a yellow cap.

16.

The water had swallowed so much
That it became drunk.
It was a whirlpool.

17.

When the fog
Had stopped
Swirling around
The falling rain
Throwing light
Fell to its knees.

18.

"I've done a world tour"
Said the man.
- Poor man
Your body hasn't
Moved an inch.

19.

The pupil
Swivelled its eyes
The iris followed it
The white of the eye
Followed slowly afterwards.
By this delay
My friend
You peer into
The face
Of your loved one.

20.

"I think
I'm a teapot"
Said the awakened madman
To the psychiatrist
"You should carry on to the end"
Answered the latter
"Where?" asked the madman
"Until you believe in Jesus and your teapot has moved."

21.

"I love you
In your yellow dress"
Said the lover.
"You're mistaken"
She said
"You love yellow.
Your compliment is to the colour."

22.

They were dancing
Suddenly the woman
Felt naked
She felt
All of a sudden
That she was beloved.

23.

Adam and Eve
Were wrong to eat the apple
They should have given it
To the serpent
Who would have died.

24.

I cover
This distance
Every day
Going to the office
- No said the other one
You swallow up time
As the steps you take
Bring you closer
To your eternity
- After all
What's that?
It's yourself.

25.

"I love you"
The woman said
"Take care
Not to love me too much"
Said the lover
"For you turn back
To yourself again.
Love is a circle."

26.

When the middle
Stretched its head
It became a circle
The circle
Retreated back into the head
And became a middle
Chop the neck
Of the remaining space
And have done with all
This geometry.

27.

Water's only prudish
When it's poured
Into a vase
And with its
Streams of water
It baptises
And opens its thighs
And circumcises.

28.

If a banana
Were hanging down
From the breast
Instead of rising to the occasion
It would be pornographic.

29.

One and one make two
Said the mathematician
That's not the case
With God and zero.

30.

A circle
Doesn't have
Reference points.
All its points
Are winning
The only loser
Is the middle.

31.

When yellow
Drank blue
It was thirsty
For red
And then
It became green.
Only the light stopped
Its thirst.

32.

The night's not black
It's invisible.
Black is the filth
Of our sins
With which it is laden.

33.

I heard
A cockerel crowing
In a leaf I had crumpled
When I looked closer
I saw
That the leaf
Was in the shape of a cockscomb.

34.

The engine whistles.
The mountain replies
What does the air do?
The air listens.
If the air spoke
You would hear nothing.

35.

If when looking at the sun
All of a sudden
You could no longer see it
You yourself would be the sun
And be reborn.

36.

Women
Have more thirst
Than hunger
In their sensual pleasure
While men
Have more hunger
Than thirst
In their relationships.

37.

In man
The mouth
Is horizontal
And sex
Is vertical
It's all part of the Golgotha
Of love.

38.

A man
Has only two joints
In his thumb.
If there were three
His hand would be too slow
To feel.

39.

He who
Faces time
Has space
Behind him.
He who
Faces space
Has time
Behind him.
Facing
Space-time
Is night.
Which no one sees.

40.

Shade
Put its back
In the water.
Its face created
The reflection.

41.

Red
Rouged its cheeks
And became a cherry.

42.

Yellow
Is always
Flabbergasted.

43.

Violet
Put paint
In its eye
And looked
Unnatural.

44.

The short grass
Made the plants
Slip.

45.

"Don't kiss me"
Said red
To yellow.
"You are going
To rub off
My rouge."

46.

The first corkscrew
Is the splinter.

47.

Red
Gripped
Green
So tightly
That it
Suffocated
And became
Black.

48.

Mauve
Is
Lukewarm.

49.

Whoever
Disrobes
Night
Sees
The body
Of God.

50.

Narcissus
Created
A postage stamp
From his reflection
In the water
And invented
Television.

51.

The leaf
Is the palm
Which
Continually
Loses its fingers
In a flower.

52.

When red
Blew its nose
Green
Nearby
Had hiccups.

53.

Space
Severs
Space:
The shadows
Intersect.

54.

What shadow
Exists
That has no fear
Of its own shadow?

55.

Raised eyelashes
Create a gladiolus
In the eye.

56.

A bell
With blue tones
Would sound the tolls
But would summon
The wings
Of angels.

57.

Iron grey
Is an obstinate
Colour.

58.

"Are you there?"
Asked the man.
"Yes" answered the woman.
"Can't you feel
My silence
Drifting towards you?"

59.

"I would like to lie down"
Said the table
- "Agreed" said the armchair
I'm your safety net.

60.

The rose
Is décolleté
Right down its back
The flower
Which reveals
Its buttocks
Is the dahlia.

61.

The dew
Is nature's
Jewel.

62.

Water is
Absolutely not
As thin as it looks.

63.

When you really want it
You can't even find
The barest bones
Of a drop of water.
The skeleton of wind
Is life.

64.

Space
Within space
Is hell.

65.

Light
Gathers up
Her skirt
To touch
The dirt.

66.

Water
Quenches its thirst
Only in the pond.

67.

Grey
Is the gown
Of evening
And of the night.

68.

Lace
Came into
The world
One frothy
Day.

69.

A pearl
Loves woman
As the moon
Loves its cycle.

70.

A badly cut diamond
Cries coloured tears.

71.

The eye
Is the theatre
Of the solitary
Actor.

72.

In the race
Of colours
The jockey
Is the one
Who has form.

73.

All the lattices
Of light
Battle with the shadows.

74.

One is
Completely in control
Of one's body
Only in death.

75.

Nothing is final
For our conscience
Never sleeps.

76.

The shadow
Assumed the form
Of a cow
Then that of a mouse
Then a plant.
I knew
From that moment
That evolution
Had never occurred.

77.

"What have you done with your life?"
Asked the plant
"I've climbed towards you
But you've never
Come towards me"
Replied the creeper.

78.

To walk on water
One must oneself
Be fire.

79.

"I'll never
Be Old"
Said the man
"I live in hope."

80.

When silence
Said nothing
The noise
Was deafening.

81.

The one that
Remains hungry
Is the earth
Which nourishes
Everything.

82.

Light
Is the richest
Of things:
She provides everything.

83.

She has decorated
Her breasts
With her eyes.

84.

Yellow is the canine tooth
Of light
Green
Is
The molars
Red
Is
The front tooth
And blue
Is
The incisors.

85.

The pearl has
Pectoral buttocks.

86.

All sexual perverts
Are grey.

87.

All leaves
Shaped like ears
Cup more beautifully
The jewelled dew drop.

88.

The road
Runs on without pause
Before allowing
The pavement to rest.

89.

Everywhere
Where roads cross
The light stops.

90.

Shade
Is the
Ever-lasting
Rendez-vous.

91.

Every woman
Who blushes
Out of modesty
Takes off her dress.

92.

In the meadow
The shade
Greets the light
With decorum
In the woods
With informality.

93.

Only water
Is a ventriloquist.

94.

The light
Which devours ceaselessly
Without diminution
Is God.
The sun
Is the bread
Of heaven.

95.

Thyme wanders
Among the lettuces
Wriggles around
The cucumbers
Flings itself
Among the parsley
And a haze of leaves
And emerges
Exhausted
In the field
Of mignonettes.

96.

In the beginning
The bear
Was a big dog
Who refused
To live among men.

97.

Religion
Is there to
Comfort
Humanity.
For all the bad things
Priests
Did to it.

98.

Water
Has two stomachs
The vase and itself.

99.

Water bathes in the nude.
But as I turn
To look
A reflection hides it.

100.

When green
Placed its hand
On yellow's shoulder
It gave a mauve shudder.

101.

The road
Is always afraid
That its turnings
Will be overwhelmed
By light.

102.

The block of ice
Was hot.
It was sweating.

103.

Hail falls seated
Hailstones fall upright
And water falls on its knees.

104.

When the fire trembled
It turned blue.
When fire is white
It is winter's light.

105.

Tears
Are those that weep the least.
The gutter sobs.

106.

Pleasure
Is the eternal
Missed rendezvous.

107.

She dined alone.
She ate herself up.

108.

The leek
Always gives
The impression
Of planting itself.

109.

Woman likes to be eaten
Man likes to be drunk.
Holy Communion takes place in bed.

110.

Blue Beard
Was impotent.

111.

"Are you rich?
- I have everything
I'm no longer in control of myself."

112.

He opened the door
To allow space to leave.
They embraced the moment
And resumed their honeymoon.

113.

When the tree felt the first blow of the axe
It leaned over towards the man
And said
"Chop the root
My friend
I don't want
To see myself
Fall."

114.

The wave
Pushed down upon
The water
And turned around.
The water took
Its place:
The air displaced
The wave
Which returned again
With the wind.

115.

The man sat
On the stone.
The stone cried out.
It was suffering.
On the other side
The sun was crushing it.

116.

Emptiness
Has
No exit.

117.

The conscience
Of a hollow
Is water.

118.

If the twelve
Had been
Crucified
With Jesus
The Christian religion
Would have been
A philosophy
With a dearth of priests.

119.

Water is hungry
For the earth
And the earth
Is thirsty for water
When the rain
Falls
We hear someone
Who swallows
And someone who chews.

120.

The gun barrel was raised
And suddenly retracted.
Earth
Had ordered
A cease-fire.

121.

If light
Adorned itself
There would have been
No room for life.

122.

When he was absolutely dead
He realised
That he hadn't
Begun
To live.

123.

He thought
So intensely
That he found himself
Outside of
His body.

124.

The grass crept
Close to the earth
When the breeze blew
It turned
Into a road again.

125.

The languid shadow
Stretched out.
Its reflection followed.

126.

If the night moved
There would be
An enormous
Earthquake.
Meanwhile
O shadow
You move!

127.

Things completely round
Create
A perfect vacuum.

128.

Space stumbles
Against time
In the debris
Of memory.

129.

All the anxiety
In repressing one's feelings
One must look for
In others.

130.

The pupil
Kneels
In ecstasy.

131.

The full
And the empty
Are at daggers drawn
In the hollow.

132.

Absolutely
Pure white
Becomes opaque
When seen transversely.

133.

Sugar
Doesn't recognise
Its taste.
The person
Who tastes it
Makes the sugar
Taste itself.

134.

The landmark
Is always
Busy
Hugging
The coast
So as not to vomit.

135.

The thread
Has no awareness
Of the cloth
Which is
Its subconscious.

136.

Bitterness
Eats alone.

137.

Water
Doesn't have
Engagements.
Its reflection
In the water
Is an unconsummated
Marriage.

138.

Shade
Is always
Impartial
No matter what
The slenderness
Or thickness
Of the object.

139.

White
Is the
Universal
Masseur.

140.

The moon
Cries
Into the pink rose
While
The sun
Laughs.

141.

Blue
Makes itself
Small
To be more
Clearly
Seen.

142.

The one-way system
Is exquisite delight.

143.

White
Teaches
The colours
How to
Take care of
Their emotions.
Red
Blushes
Inside
The rose.

144.

The stems of
The bamboo
In motion
Are its crutches.

145.

If one suppressed
Time
Space
Would become
The ultimate
Atomic bomb
And destroy
The universe.

146.

All metallic noises
Sound like
Sick animals.

147.

The stone
Hears its
Heartbeat
Only when
It rains.

148.

The flying
Dust
Is blinded
By the eyelashes
Of light.

149.

Blend
The butter
And you will see
Quite unintentionally
The emerging
Movements
Of the cow.

150.

Electricity
Doesn't
Question itself
Unduly
On how
To find
Its place.

151.

The circle
Is obsessed
By the centre
And the centre
Intoxicated by the circle
Snookers them
And creates the line.

152.

The misfortune
Of youth
Is to see
Life
Grow old.

153.

The breast
Was thirsty
For its milk.
It drank.
A pearl appeared.

154.

All women
Are unfaithful
To their husbands
With their dresses.

155.

"My thought
Doesn't belong
To me"
Said water
"The air has stolen it."
....
The breeze paused
And the water saw
That the breeze
Was considering it.

156.

A woman's sex
Has loyalty
To no one.

157.

Colours
Are the strings
Of the puppets
Of space.

158.

A circle
Is the centre's
Alibi
And the centre
Is the circle's
Excuse.

159.

Throughout the night
Without the sun
All creatures
Are shadows.

160.

Shade
Is the echo
Of light.

161.

All flowers
Spit out
Their eyebrows
In splinters.

162.

All colours
Held
Too closely
Escape
In entirety.

163.

The moon
Dribbles
Its mouth
In the water.

164.

The lovers
Listen to themselves
As they breathe.

165.

Every glance
Begins
To grow old
During the tempest.

166.

Death
In nature
Turns
Grey.

167.

Sleeping water
Dreams
Of its reflection.

168.

Oil is
Engaged
In close combat
That's why
It runs
So slowly.

169.

Blue petals
Show their
Pink gums
When the rose
Mingles with
The blueberries
Among the lilies.

170.

The light brown colour
Has spots.

171.

Eyelashes
Are
The candlestick
Of observation.

172.

The rose
Seems
Always astonished
To be a rose.

173.

In the stare
That burns
The ember
Is boredom.

174.

Colour
Is a dress
Without
An underskirt.

175.

Shape
Is
The speed-change
Of colours.

176.

Buttocks
Answer
To nobody.

177.

The echo
Ate itself.
Space
Had spoken.

178.

The mirror
Is never
Outspoken.
It doesn't have
An opinion.

179.

Women
Listen
With
Their mouths.

180.

Fire
Never catches
Fire.
The flame
Is the air
Blazing
Around its
Cold heart.

181.

Shade
Commits
No faux-pas.

182.

White
Commits
Hari-kiri
Among
The harlequin
Colours.

183.

If all
The clouds of dust
In the world
Were In harmony
They would
Turn the mountains
Topsy-turvy.
Mud is the
Middle ground.

184.

In bronzing
Blue
Is the cuckold.

185.

Brown
Is always
Unwell.

186.

An idea
Is an image
That can't decide
Between
Memory and imagination.

187.

The canal
Made a queue.
In the pipe
The water
Awaits its turn.

188.

The film
Said to the image
"Don't go so quickly
Or I'll catch fire."
....
The actual film
Was in colour.

189.

All colours
Appear shady
When seen
From the side.
Coming together
Changes them.

190.

Grey
Is a mist
Of colours
Which merges
Into black.

191.

Blue sipped
Yellow's cup.
Milk
Was the white.
The cup
Empty of its white
Was then
Only a cup
Swallowed up
By milky-blue.

192.

Moonlight
Is
Milky yellow.

193.

All colours
Lose their breath
In white.

194.

All clouds
Imagine the sea.
Not a single fish
Imagines the ocean.

195.

He thought so intensely
He saw
His own idea.
It resembled
The image
Of his face
It was himself.

196.

All mirrors
Lie
Because they reflect
What they do not see.

197.

The shortest way
From ourselves
To ourselves
Is the universe.

198.

The machine
Is always
Afraid of
Its own roar.

199.

Water
In a vase
Doesn't see
The vase.
It sees
The shape of the vase
And believes that it is itself.

200.

In the shower
Water takes a bath
With bad grace.

201.

Beige
Is one's ideal armchair.

202.

All colours
Are friendly
With their neighbours
And love
To be face to face.

203.

Coral is
A white club foot.

204.

Passer by
Why do you hurry so?
You stumble over yourself.
Only infinity
Has no space.

205.

I pulled
The string
On the floor
And saw
The floor move.
Don't be alarmed
You're not crazy
You've just seen
The other side
Of yourself.

206.

Woman
Always forgets
Her buttocks
She's too occupied
With her breasts.

207.

The most lovely fan
Is the mouth
It opens
In the middle.

208.

Blue
Always
Has an idea
In the back
Of its mind.

209.

Snub yellow
And it becomes white.

210.

Sea water
Always
Pulls off
Its trousers
To jump over
The reef.

211.

Water was afraid
Of getting wet
And became
Mist.

212.

If mankind
Made love
Together
The feeling
Of happiness
Would be endless.

213.

White
Is never
Colourless.

214.

Black
Is perforated
Light.

215.

Light
Laces up
The plants'
Shoes.

216.

Only yellow
Arrives on time.

217.

Water must
Never touch fire
- ? ! ? ! ! ?
It would put out
The sun.

218.

She loved him
So much
That one day
She thought
She had become
His husband.
- What happened?
- The man became mad.

219.

She put on
Her dress
And then the blue of
Her dress
And then went
To a rendezvous
With her lover.
And when she returned?
- She had lost
Her dress
She had kept
The blue.
- And then?
- Each time
She wasn't in a blue
Dress
She felt
Disrobed.

220.

A rainbow?
It's the necklace
Searching
For its neck.

221.

A diamond
Is eternally drowning
Where its dimension
Dictates
Artificial respiration.

222.

Jesus touched
The blind man's eyes
And the blind man could see.
And then looking
At his own hands
He saw that they
Were made of light.

223.

All buttocks
Sway
Right and left.

224.

A hole in a hole
Is full.

225.

She came
And gave herself.
Then she left
Leaving part of
Herself on the bed.
The man absorbed her
Under his skin.

226.

The animals
In the ark
Were the idea
Of Noah.

227.

Yellow putty
Constipates.

228.

Light
Is only truly
Naked
At the water's
Edge.

229.

The egg white
Said to the yolk
"You are my antipodes."

230.

The squaring of
The circle
Is the vision
At the bosom
Of the look.

231.

Eve
Carried
Her sex
In her mouth.
Quickly followed
By her modesty.

232.

Mirrors
Have
No memory.

233.

The fading rose
Is ageless.

234.

A needle
That pricks another
Is the splinter
Of a diamond.

235.

Every root
Above the soil
Scampers
Like a bird.

236.

She's burning up
With worry.
Who is she?
The grey
Of raw silk.

237.

Green
Is the colour
Which lasts
The best.
Blue
Forms parasols.

238.

Colours
Are not
Half-bloods.

239.

Mauve
Weeps
Silver tears
And laughs
With golden smiles.

240.

Space
Lost
Its pocket
But found it
In a seed.

241.

The sick
Banana
Had
A whitlow.

242.

Night
Has no dormitory
She sleeps
Wherever she wants.

243.

Water
Has
Trousers
Of foam.

244.

The tired machine
Snored.
Time
Was asleep
In her bosom.

245.

The tropical bird
Is an orchid
That searches
For its wings
In the light.

246.

The pips
In the grape
Play a game
Of golf
Without holes.

247.

The light
Sheds its leaves
When
Autumn petals
Fall.

248.

All bleak
Noises
Feel
The waves.

249.

Not one
Perfume is pure.

250.

Belief
Is the weariness
Of believers.

251.

Oil
Never glides
Along
So well
As when
It is
Braking.

252.

Every mountain
Has the easy-chair
It deserves.

253.

The white bald head
Is the bone.

254.

All blazing blues
Have their
Throats constricted
By love.

255.

The spider
Died
When
It saw
The fly.

256.

Don Juan
Became a mystic
To avoid
Being
A homosexual.

257.

If mothers
Had pointed breasts
Later on
The child
Wouldn't be able
To suck its thumb.

258.

Lilac
Is the rose
That dreams.

259.

On the day of reckoning
The cockerel
Crowed at the moon
And then
The dog
Barked at the sun.

260.

The cheeks
Are looking
For cheek
In the smile.

261.

The creeper
Is the perfect
Gymnast.

262.

All words
Are flytraps.
The spider
Is the idea.

263.

The bank
Is a bleak
Custom.

264.

Don't force
The fire.
It goes out.

265.

The Aurora Borealis
Is the breath
Of the light
Facing
Intense cold.

266.

She squinted so badly
That she dislocated
Her hip.

267.

The grass had
A cold
And said to the air:
"Pass me
Your handkerchief
My darling!"

268.

The night
Is a hole
Without edges.

269.

The barley-sugar
Lost its tongue
From the sheer
Intensity
Of its sucking.

270.

A star
Slipped
In the sky.
Space surrendered.
Time was falling.

271.

The light
Put on a corset
To defend itself
Against the reverberation.

272.

The lilies
Froze space
With their
White cries.
There came
A red bird
Which bled
Into the white.
Summer was snowing.

273.

Everything
Scattered
First and foremost
Not to be eaten.
Only
The earth
That eats all
And that all
Eat
Defends itself.

274.

Water
In water
Is light.

275.

This evening
Night
Slept alone:
She'd been
Put
In the cellar.

276.

The water caressed
Bare-footed blue.
It made
A big green ripple
On the sea.

277.

The sea
Had opened
Her thighs
And one
Was aware
Of the smell
Of algae.

278.

The surface of aloes
Is
A failed artichoke.

279.

Silence
Covered its ears.
The atom bomb
Fell.

280.

The movement
Of water
Is an
Everlasting thirst.

281.

Oblivion
Had a fainting fit
And found itself
Extinguished
In the gardens
Of memory.

282.

Appetite
Was
So hungry
It ate itself up.

283.

Between them
One's two lips
Are in
A mutual
Perpetual kiss.

284.

The line
Fussed around
On the spot
And in the act
It created the circle.
The centre
Was born.

285.

Yellow
Gave
The blue oil
A bit of garlic.

286.

He gave himself
Such airs
That he never realised
His body
Was making fun
Of him.

287.

The eye
Bulged
And gave birth
To a stillborn:
How ridiculous.

288.

She gave.
He accepted.
The third person
Was time
Who made
Cuckolds
Of them both.

289.

The branch
Tucked its knees
Under its neck
And saved itself
In the creeper.

290.

Light
Has space
For a
Bathroom.

291.

Colours
Are not
Always
Old.
Their shapes
Age them.

292.

The grey smoke
Puffed out
A blue smile.
The fire was
Bored.

293.

At midday
Light
Has its
Riding lesson.

294.

Perspective
Is
Non-transformative
Rubber.

295.

The mountain range
Went so fast
That the road
Had
Only
Just enough time
To twist around it.

296.

The nape
Is
The dormitory
Of the neck.

297.

The thigh
Was violated.
The sex
Is always
Consensual.

298.

The road
Runs
In both directions
That's why
It doesn't move.

299.

The
Fire's
Fixed gaze
Caused
Its extinction.

300.

The watch
Is slower
Than its case.

301.

Every hat
Makes
A second head.

302.

The necklace
Said to the neck:
"Don't squeeze me
Too tightly.
You are suffocating me."

303.

All madmen
Would be healed
If they could be
Made to face
Their doubles.

304.

For a camel
To pass
Through the eye
Of a needle
It needs only
To be filmed
Backwards.

305.

Sound
Hears itself
Only
In its echo.

306.

Prince Charming
Didn't marry
Sleeping Beauty
He took her
As his mistress.

307.

A car
Is only conscious
Of itself
When in a collision.

308.

The balloon
Sulked so much
It burst.

309.

Silence
Was suddenly halted
By an inner-sound
Then the piano
Became
A ventriloquist.

310.

Fortune
Said to luck:
"Let's get married
And perform miracles."

311.

The light was tired
Having read too much.
The man's eyes closed.

312.

The fire
Having destroyed
Everything
Looked at himself
Terror stricken.
He knew that he
Was going to
Destroy himself
And that would
Be the end of him.

313.

The white horses
Gallop up
The sea's foam
Beneath their hooves.

314.

The shattered rock
Checked out
Its bones.

315.

The large plants
Rippled in the breeze.
The fish
In the sea
Popped up its head
And upon seeing
The hillside
Said:
"Who depopulated
This place?"

316.

The clasp
Closing
The door
Realised
It was imprisoned
By the door.
The man opened it
And the clasp
Became prisoner
Of its freedom.

317.

The creeper
In love with
The tree trunk
Said to it:
"Make room
For me
You are in me
And I can't hold you."

318.

The fern
Smoothed her hair
After the wind
Had combed it.

319.

The wall
In front of
The posters
Causes their distress
As we look on.

320.

The electric wire
Travelled so quickly
That it made
The poles
Vanish.

321.

All buttocks
Are lying
Under their
White coverings.

322.

The sex
Of light
Is hidden
By shadow.

323.

The gate
Asked itself
If space
Passes through
Or follows it.

324.

The door
Exists
So that the wall
Doesn't pass
Through everything.

325.

The geranium
And its roots
Were the anchors
Of shade.

326.

The film
Floating on the water
Is its coverlet.

327.

The stream
Ran so quickly
That the trees
Following
Were not able
To catch up with it
Until it reached
The sea.

328.

Shadow
Makes a seesaw
Of everything.

329.

The knife
Cut itself.
Then came the meal.

330.

In order
To let the door
Go by
The window
Passed through it.

331.

Space
Props up everything
And rests
On nothing.

332.

Sensual pleasure
Is at the centre
Of the cyclone
Of the senses.

333.

The boulder
Showed
Its coccyx
When it shattered.

334.

The water
Lost its footing
As the last
Drop
Of water
Evaporated.

335.

The boundary stone
Always thought of
Itself
As being
The beginning
Of the road.

336.

The mud
Used the earth
As a table
And dined
On rubbish.

337.

The illuminated poster
Was waiting for someone:
The day.

338.

The corner
Was looking
Both ways:
"No accident?"
It said.
The corner
Was bored.

339.

The tulip
Lifted her dress
To hide
Her buttocks.

340.

The staircase
Climbed
With large steps.
When it reached
The top
All the steps
Came tumbling
Down.

341.

White
Always wears
A night shirt.
Lifts up the
Nightshirt
To colourlessness.
Lift this colourlessness
To present the night.

342.

They walked alone.
They displaced
Space
With their breath
And time
With their words.

343.

The lock
Is always
Trying to find
A way out
Using the key.

344.

The water
Was frightened
And swallowed itself.
The wind
Practised artificial
Respiration on it
And the water
Revived.

345.

Silence
Became
Voiceless.

346.

Tapping
Its foot
Against a rock
The child
Heard the rock
Say:
"Who's hitting
My heart
With a soft
Hammer?"

347.

Laughter
Could laugh
No more.
It said to the
Tear:
"Help me."

348.

White
Put itself
On a diet of colours
In order to slim.

349.

The syncope
Of the wheel
Which revolves
Is the night
Moving forward
By its vanishing.

350.

The whirlwind
Is water
With a crick in the neck.

351.

"I'm thirsty," said the bread.
"I'm hungry," said the water.
They came together.

352.

The blotting paper
Said to the ink:
"You're copying me."

353.

The dog
Barked
At the moon
Because he
Thought
It was
A bone.

354.

The pin was so
Sensitive
It suffered when
It pricked
The paper.

355.

Electricity
Was
Coming and going
To find out
Where it came from.

356.

Grease
Is false
Fat.

357.

The man
Saw himself
In the mirror
In such a fashion
That he
Lost sight of himself.

358.

The orchid
Puts her hands
In her pockets
Then looks for them
Everywhere.

359.

Anyone able
Simultaneously
To see both ends
Of the Antipodes
Would be in the sun
From where the earth
Has no depth.

360.

All natural shapes
Are the clothes
Of man's body.

361.

The worst kind
Of blindness
Is the grey
Seen in the black.

362.

In order to catch
The centre
One must grasp
The circle.
But as
The number of circles
Is infinite
One never reaches
The centre.
Infinity
Is on the point
Of nothingness.

363.

Trot
Oh dog
Like a deer
With its ears
To the wind.
I cry out to you
And I see you
Changed into
A cat
With velvet paws.

364.

Light's theme
Is a lily
A pistol
Of fire.

365.

The shadow
Has never
Seen the sun
For the sun
Has no shadow.

366.

Colours
Are the most
Consistent
Of all things.

367.

Love
Makes us
Anticipate
The look
Before
The eyes do.

368.

When the water
Had lost
Its mouth
It looked at itself.
Its mouth
Was under the water:
Shining.

369.

The water
Was so thirsty
It went
To drink
In the lonely creeks
Of deserts of water
Of boundless seas.

370.

Night
Seen
In full daylight
Is colourless.

371.

The buttocks
Are an armchair
Sitting
On a cushion.

372.

Rain
Was afraid
Of catching a cold
So wrapped itself
In mist.

373.

Night
Is always
In bed.

374.

Every woman
Is an atheist
When it comes
To her sex.

375.

The marguerite
Makes
Pretty little hands
Of the eyes.

376.

The drop of blood
Drank its blood
And sweated.

377.

The egg
Rolled.
Its hands
Clung to
Its belly.

378.

The weeds
Creep
Towards
The crutches
Of shade.

379.

The geese
Advance
As a gaggle
Of buttocks
In the sun.

380.

The window
Wiped its eyes
With the handkerchief
Of the curtain.
It was raining.

381.

In every way
Light assists
In its burial
By the shadows.

382.

The diamond
Created
A bib
In the ring.

383.

The light
Played
Leapfrog
With the shadows.
Its last leap
Was into
This bouquet
Of roses
Where it
Was crushed
Into shards.

384.

The eye
Had a stiff neck
On the luminescent
Nape
Of the dazzling
Fountain.

385.

The mire of clarity
Was full of
Luminous brilliance.

386.

Mauve
Fell
And developed
A bump.
It was a pearl.

387.

The dress
Dressed herself
With her ribbons.

388.

The breeze
Shook
The foliage.
On the earth
There was a
A tremor of light.

389.

Space
Breathed
So strongly
That the echo
Swallowed it up.

390.

The book
Tired
Of reading to itself
Fell asleep.
Its thoughts
Snored
In the reading room.

391.

All the crossed lights
Appeared to be
Dreaming.

392.

This morning
The light on the sea
Had donned
Its slippers.
The foam
Was afraid
Of getting wet.

393.

The mud
Always
Believed
The water
Wanted to
Make it dirty.

394.

Every skylight
Looks the
Wrong way
When the sun
Turns.

395.

The mouth
Resented
The cheek
And the cheek
Resented
The mouth.
Laughter threw them
Into the arms of
One another.

396.

He came backwards
And collided with
His thought
Which was
In front of him.

397.

The ring
Always
Thought
Himself to be
The finger's
Reason for living.

398.

The carpet
Trod quickly.
Someone trod
On it.
It stopped
To see how
To pass
The footprint.

399.

The handrail
Felt dizzy
And fell
Into the
Spiral staircase.

400.

A spiral
Is ageless
In its infinity.

401.

The astonished ladle
Thought it had
Touched a breast
In the soup.

402.

The chair
Always
Believed itself
To be
The most important
Person seated.

403.

White
Became
Sluggish
In silver.

404.

The tyre was
Always
Convinced
That the rubber
Was the road.

405.

The window pane
Didn't know
On which side
To look
So as to
Recognise itself.

406.

The hole
Emerging
From its
Hole
Left
An obstructed
Passage.

407.

The perfect dish
Fell because
It wasn't
Held properly.

408.

The telescope
Is
The tower of Babel
Which has touched
The sky.

409.

The leaves
In the breeze
Create
A masked ball
In the forest.

410.

One nail
Said to the other:
"You are
My flint."

411.

The diamond
In its prison
Of light
Felt that
It was enveloped
In streamers.

412.

The room
Full of furniture
Didn't know
Where to go.

413.

The road
Became shorter
At the bend.
Space had
Rotated.

414.

Space
Is merely
A wall
Which moves forward.
The object
Of atomism
Is
To break down
This wall.

415.

The robe
Raised itself
The thigh
Lowered
From the waist
And revealed
Its sex
It was
The hem.

416.

The route
Believed
It was a post
And crashed
Into
The car.

417.

The water
Massaged
Itself
So well
Before
Dropping
That
In the deluge
It was only
A bag of bones.

418.

The full
Tide
Felt
Seasick.

419.

The point
Is the only
Object
Content
With its
Place.

420.

She was
Naked
Only when
Enjoying
Sensual pleasure.

421.

Space
Considered
Asking
Who had
Placed
It
There.

422.

The moonraker
On the coconut tree
Believed that the
Palm tree
Wasn't moving
Because
Its colour
Was fanning itself.

423.

All water
Runs
To create
A slope
To balance
Its water level.

424.

Oil
Was tossed
Onto water.
And water
So as not
To overflow
Lay on its
Back.

425.

The gears
Broke
Its teeth
Chewing
Too vigorously
On the movement.

426.

The dust
In the air
Sneezed
And swallowed
So much wind
That it was
Thrown
To earth.

427.

Light
Bathed
At the edge
Of the water.
A shadow
Passed
And flung it
In the water.

428.

This morning
The cloud
Dropped
Its umbrella.

429.

The cinder
On the ground
Asked itself
Where has the
Fire gone?
The smoke
Replied:
"You swallowed it."

430.

The brassiere
And the G-string
Both thought
They were hidden
Because they were
Transparent.

431.

Water
Full of air
Began
To burp.

432.

Yellow
Hitting against
Violet
Had a blue
Bruise.
The azurian canopy
Was created.

433.

The shoulder
Gave the hip
A hair style.

434.

When
The fog
Opened
Its eyes
It saw
That everyone
Was looking
At it.

435.

Every virgin
Has a penis
In her voice.

436.

The skull
At the bottom
Of the tomb
Laughed
At the excellent
Joke
He'd played
On everyone.

437.

The water
Lacking
Soap
Took the earth
And wiped
Itself down.

438.

The mouth
Was bedridden
The eye stayed
Sitting up.

439.

All buttocks
Resemble one another
On the
Chamber-pot.

440.

Black
Was
So frightened
It turned
Grey.

441.

In formal
French
Gardens
It's the light
That does
All the work.

442.

The bridge
Arrived from the
Other end
Realised
It was being
Driven round the bend
Turned and went the way it came.
It overtook
Itself.

443.

The oyster
Swallowed
Its pearl
And turned
Into
A pearly
Butterfly.

444.

The eyelid
Vanished
Into thin air.
Its gaze
Floated away.

445.

The glue
All ensnared
In its clumsiness
Was overcome
By emotion
For the paper
And loved it
With an unwavering
Heart.

446.

In order
To render
Bird-lime
Pliable
One must
Soften it
With one's
Fingers.

447.

The light
Lost its eyes.
Darkness
Fell.

448.

The moon
Was shivering.
The sun
Ironed it.

449.

It was raining.
The air
Had forgotten
Its overcoat.

450.

The low-cut
Cleavage
Created a thigh
Where the neck
Should have been.

451.

The lampshade
Laughed
Under its robe
Of light.

452.

In eternity
Night doesn't
Exist.
Colours
Sound
The hours.

453.

Hard mouths
Like
Soft hats.

454.

At midday
Shade makes
An orphan
Of the sun.

455.

The hedge
Ran between the legs
Of the wind
It stopped
And the air
Wrapped its legs
Around its neck.

456.

Time feeling itself
Grow old
Ate itself up
And was rejuvenated.

457.

The buttered bread
Was hungry
The man was
No longer hungry.

458.

All that is removed
From the motionless night
Catches fire.

459.

Colours
Only
Laugh
When
It
Rains.

460.

To conceal its sex
Perfume took a stroll
Naked
In the form
Of a flower.

461.

The water
Had fasted
So much
That on
Its descent
It was no more
Than a bag of bones.

462.

The post wanted
To follow
The path
In the shade
And fell
Into the canal.

463.

The terrestrial globe
Moved no more.
The night
Was meditating.

464.

A rock
Made a hole
At the water's edge
And drank up
The anus of the waves.

465.

The eye
Beneath the hat
Fluttered its eyelashes.

466.

Naked grey
Wearing a nightgown
Became invisible.

467.

The light
Smoothed down
The moustache
In the heart
Of this delicate
Fern.

468.

The moon
That evening
Slept so badly
The clouds
Were giving it
Nightmares.

469.

Winter had caught a cold.
This winter
The snow was sneezing.

470.

All the
Roughly-handled
Martyrised metals
Contain the cries
Of the wounded.

471.

The octopus
Moves
Using its tentacles
Leaning on
The crutches of water.

472.

The light
Bathed its eyes
In the sea.
It rained
Heavily.

473.

The lightning wanted
To come before night
Thunder came first.

474.

The air
Vitrified the window
It shattered
Like
An 'H' bomb.

475.

Dots never vanish.
He who
Draws a line
Begins from
A stationary
Position.

476.

The light
Embarrassingly tripped
Lost its footing
And fell into
The wrong day.

477.

Air is
The earth's toilet.

478.

The boulder
Walked with small steps
Among
The chippings
And broke its foot
Under the wheel of the car.

479.

Light
Having
Given back
Its chemise
Turned
Black.

480.

The stone
Fell
Into the water
The water
Quickly covered
The fallen stone
With its skirt.

481.

The open eyes
Under the black hair
Said to the eyelashes:
"Lower
Your awning
My beloved
I can be seen
Too clearly
From the road."

482.

The sparkle
Was lost
From sight.
When it revived
It was night time
And it was
Mistaken
For a star.

483.

The root
Was searching
Underground
For
The origin
Of the tree.

484.

When the mud
Took a bath
It dried out.

485.

"Take me naked"
The flower said
To the sun
"Before the night
Closes
My thighs."

486.

As with a handkerchief
She mislaid
Her hips
Everywhere.
They were returned
To her
Along with
Some love letters.

487.

God will never
Arrive
At a conclusion.
He is continually
Sub-dividing.

488.

The vinegar
Had
A bad stomach
Because it drank
Too much oil.

489.

The deflated wheel
Had a contraction
Of
The axle.

490.

The bowl
Fed up with being stirred
Spewed the spoon
Over
The handle.

491.

Summer
Passed so quickly
That Autumn
Caught it
In the leaves and flowers.

492.

The light
Wore
A yellow robe
To woo
Lilac.

493.

All colours dine
At the same
Yellow table.

494.

The eye
Is lost
In wonder
When the mouth
Smiles.

495.

The night raced along
So quickly
During the night
That when daybreak came
It had
Exhausted
Its speed and space.

496.

When the rose blushed
It turned
White
With happiness.

497.

The oleander
Had moved
So quickly
Along its path
That when
Day dawned
The shadow
Saw the oleander
Had
Circled the globe.

498.

In the meadow
Where the trees
Run
The grass
Always wins.

499.

Clarity of thought
Had been blocked
By the vibrations
Of the light.

500.

The piece of elastic
Was measuring itself.
The light
Was flexing
Its muscles.

501.

Summer was so hot
That it
Sweated out
Large droplets
Of rain.

502.

Light turns its back only once:
At death.

503.

Earth sleeps
At midday
And awakens
The night.

504.

The road
Had corns
From walking
Too much.

505.

He was
So dignified
That he
Wasn't aware
That his body
Was making fun
Of him.

506.

The wet grass
Rinsed its fingers
In the bowl
Of light.

507.

Sound crunched
Its teeth
And left them
In the keys
Of the piano.

508.

Centrifuge
And centripetal
Exist
To compromise
The night.

509.

The tortoise travels
So slowly
Because it is
In love
With its feet.

510.

Time had forgotten
The time
On the clock.

511.

The flea believed
The mountain
Would turn
Topsy-turvy
When its
Shadows reversed.

512.

The ground
Unearthed itself.
The car
Which climbed
The slope
Revived it.

513.

The coal went into
A black room
To see the light
More clearly.

514.

Brown took
The yellow
Canary
As a purgative.

515.

Many
Pieces of cloth
Are made of
Eyelashes
And the spider
Is the eye.

516.

The house walked
All around
The veranda.

517.

The sausage
Pulled in
Its stomach
So that it felt
Less hungry.

518.

The mango
Tippled its chin
With its cheek.

519.

The serpent
Had diarrhoea
Followed by
Its intestines.

520.

The tree
Escaped into
Its branches
Before greeting
The passing breeze.

521.

The cloud
Cried
Because it had
Drunk
Too much.

522.

The advancing trees
Kept clear
Of the waves
Of grass.

523.

The shade itself
Nailed down
Its coffin
In the hole.

524.

Looking in the mirror
The eye
Powdered itself
While the eyelashes
Brushed off
The excess.

525.

One day
Someone
Invented an ear
And made
A corkscrew.

526.

The full moon
Created
A child
In the water.

527.

The quicklime
Rid itself of black
So that
It could
See better.

528.

The hip
Trundled
The cart
Of its body
Where it was sitting.

529.

The smoke
Caught fire
In a
Soap bubble.

530.

She wore
Her sex
Like a charm
Hanging
Between
Her breasts.

531.

Speed
Stole a march
On speed
Along the line
It was following.

532.

Her eyelashes
Could no longer see
Because of baldness
In the white of her eye.

533.

The fire
Caught fire
And became
A blaze of colour.

534.

The rock
Broke
In two
To be familiar
With its lament.

535.

In the moonlight
Pearls shine
Like diamonds.

536.

The tap
Next to
The red handkerchief
Pissed blood.

537.

The fire
Having caught a cold
Fashioned a mantilla
Out of
The moist air.

538.

Blue jumped.
Yellow
Had given it
A nip.

539.

This morning
Sensuality
Was ill.
Las night
She was married.

540.

The sun
Lost
Its claws
In the hollows.

541.

The roof
Escaped
Into the chimney.

542.

The oil
Vomited
When
The water
Burned
Its stomach.

543.

The cross
Wanted to escape
From the tomb.
Death
Reopened it.
It was its shadow.

544.

Rain lost
All its eyelashes
Because it cried
So much.

545.

The full moon
Is the sun's
Buttocks.

546.

The brown flea
Has enteritis.

547.

The mirror
Is the everlasting
Idle onlooker.

548.

Night Falls.
Space shuts
Its doors.

549.

The finest cockerel
Is the one
Which doesn't
Make the
Chickens
Run away.

550.

The spider
Put on its
Wedding veil
To marry
The fly.

551.

The sea
Took its bath
Wearing
A bathing suit
Of algae.

552.

The lily
Removed her girdle.
The dahlia
Kissed her
Between
The thighs.

553.

The water went
To paddle barefoot
In the sea.

554.

The mountain
Took
Her knickers off
To piss
On the plain.

555.

Blue blocked
The route
To the horizon.

556.

She was always
Sitting down higher
Than her buttocks.

557.

He had
The deplorable
Habit
Of walking
Like a tree:
With each step
He uprooted himself.

558.

Colour was
So hungry
That it ate up
The shadow.

559.

Her eyes
Were moving
So quickly
That her mouth
Was able
To take
Two mouthfuls
At a time.

560.

The pillow
Sucked its thumb
In the corner
Of the sheet
And sipped
The night.

561.

She ate her mouth
While thinking
Of her eyes.

562.

She purified
Her soul
By purging
Her gowns.

563.

The eye
Was sitting
At the table.
The white of the eye
Served up the pupil
In the vessel
Of the iris.

564.

The pearl cried
For the light
Which dried
Its eyes.

565.

There was
So much
Noise that evening
That night
Couldn't sleep.
Morning saw it
Under the table
And woke it.

566.

The small birds
Learned the rudiments
Of music
With the colours
Of springtime.

567.

The light
Had
A cold
In the brain.
The sun
Sneezed
Because of
The reverberation.

568.

The water
Let its
Sprinkler drop
Then followed
After.

569.

The fish
Projected
Its colours.

570.

The look in her eye
Was in the handbag
Of her mouth.

571.

There were
Splinters of light
On the window pane.
Space was squinting.

572.

The setting having sun
Sent its shadows
Far and wide
To delay the
Oncoming night.

573.

Light
Tried
In vain
To chew up
All the holes
Which had placed
The observations
Of man
Into space.

574.

Honey
Sucked itself
And became
Bitter.

575.

The way she walked
Enveloped her.

576.

Through modesty
The water clenched
Its buttocks.
The oar
Passed over
And left it
Unsullied.

577.

The rock
Which had been raked up
Advanced
Like a lobster
Among the waves
Of dead leaves.

578.

The lines of cypresses
Bore
The road's
Coffin.

579.

Massive blue
Became
Large blue.

580.

Each morning
White's alarm clock
Rang.

581.

The midday
Shadows
Were
The pall-bearers
That turned
The ashes
To dust.

582.

Water
Had drunk
So much
That it became
Gaseous.

583.

Echo
Became deaf.
Water was
Pounding out
Its sound.

584.

The awakening
Sleeping Beauty
Charmed
The Prince
To sleep.

585.

Her smile
Was pegged
To her teeth.

586.

After the wedding
The flower's breath
Changed into
The breath of fruit.

587.

The eye of the light
Dozed between
The eyelashes
Of the ferns.

588.

The ember
Like a large cigar
Smoked
Its own pipe
At the other end.

589.

The water
Fiddled
With its breasts
In the reflection
Of a pear.

590.

Midday
Puts
The shade
To bed.

591.

The road
Rumbled along
The grass
Enabling
Each car
To pass
More easily.

592.

The eye
Had to blow
Its nose
Because
It had laughed
So much.

593.

The light in
Her afternoon dress
Went to play golf
With the holes.

594.

The water was lively.
Its own kisses
Were dappling it with joy.

595.

The two women
Judged one another
By their breasts.

596.

Jacob's ladder
Was the rainbow.

597.

In the company
Of the flea
Grey
Was the irritant.

598.

The peppermint
Had toothache
When it touched
Hot food.

599.

The wheat
In the oven
Of the sun
Baked its
Own bread.

600.

In order to recover
From good and bad
He made his peace
With both sides.

601.

The geraniums
Held hands
While strolling
Along the path
Which gave them
Great pleasure.

602.

The fountain
Moved to tears
Head in water
Saw the basin weep.

603.

Light
In the mud
Had diarrhoea.

604.

She prettied herself up
To make herself
Look younger.

605.

The dancer
Glided on her
Toes
Like a lily.

606.

This morning
The lake
Having had
A bad night
Took a bath
In order
To relax.

607.

Light hurt
Its eye
And created
The gladiolus.

608.

The wave
Lost its footing
On the shore
And sank.

609.

The house
Sitting on its bottom
Peered through
The skylight
When the doors were opened
It
Came down.

610.

The eternal
Pederast
Is
The mattress.

611.

Letters
Still
Have to learn
The alphabet.

612.

The sun
Enveloped
By the lapping waves
Turned into
Golden rings.

613.

Whilst awaiting
Something better
Sex
Fondled
Its own hairs.

614.

The stone
Had aching bones.
Someone
Had battered it.

615.

The shop
Strode around
The counters
And sat
At each
Entrance door.

616.

The woman
Remembered
That she had
Thighs
When she had
Them open.

617.

Together
The holes
Paid a visit
To the fallen
Darkness.

618.

The prison
Unshackled
By its walls
Didn't dare
Escape.
The prisoners
Restrained it.

619.

The path went
Towards the road
To see if anyone
Was coming.

620.

The shoe
Gave itself
A kick
Then it put on
Soft slippers.

621.

She made cider
With her hips
And harvested her breasts.

622.

The round-a-bout
Rooted Zeno
To the spot
And began circling
Around him.

623.

She walked
Like a wardrobe.

624.

The barrier
And the car
Were having a race.
The car was
The referee.

625.

The dog
Turned into
A cat
In front of
The small
Child.

626.

The wet rain
Dripped
Into
The pond.

627.

The floor
Was pacing
Up and down.
When the door
Opened
It left
The room.

628.

The incline
Made the car
Breathe heavily.

629.

The church moved
Towards the crowd
Which was moving
Towards it.

630.

She resembled
A large pineapple
As she balanced
On her haunches.

631.

Her garlic caresses
Her mouth
Of vinegar
But her eyes
Were
Like honey.

632.

She
Sat
Like a
Stool.

633.

The door
Entered
By the entrance
And left
When the man
Had passed through.

634.

The water
Was not
On speaking terms
With the oar.

635.

The marquee
Climbed
On the roof
In search of
Its head.

636.

Space
Made
A mistake
And created
A hole.

637.

The cloud
Hid itself
From the rain
In its tent.

638.

The drop
Of water
On the table
- Soaked
To the skin -
Dried itself up.

639.

The exquisite delight
Quavered.
The couple
Had undressed
Too soon.

640.

The horse's
Imprints
In the mud
Regained
The road
On foot.

641.

The spider
Went
Under the mosquito net
Because of
The flies.

642.

She crawled
Out of bed
On her haunches.

643.

The pear
Created a child
Out of an apple
In the apricot.

644.

The water
Which was
Coming
Head first
Set off
Under the bridge
By foot.

645.

She pulled
Her back
In all directions
Trying to adjust
Her buttocks
Under her dress.

646.

The stone
Ate its own buttocks
From being
Seated
So long.

647.

The rain fell
When the
Large stones
Were no longer
Able to perspire.

648.

Plants eat sparingly
In the evening
So they
Can sleep well.

649.

She undressed
Like someone
Lifting
A curtain.

650.

It's so as
To avoid
The slope
That the
Water runs.

651.

The carrot
Gobbled up
The horse's mouth
Which
Was eating
Its nose.

652.

The cockerel
Devoid of teeth
Pecked the
Ear of corn
Before
Putting in
Its dentures.

653.

The mirror
Doesn't have
A heart
But plenty
Of ideas.

654.

The eye
Knocked
At the door
And the mouth
Came in.

655.

Every time
She bent down
She used
Her eyes
Like a brassiere.

656.

The smoke
Smoked
Its own shadow.

657.

The tree
Without an overcoat
Ran in the rain
In search of
The wind.

658.

Blue
Moved
Towards the ocean
Using the water
To balance.

659.

They served up
The same course
For both the table
And the bed.

660.

The cherry
She was eating
Full of joy
Said to her:
"Eat me whole
In order to have
My image inside you."

661.

So tired
Of going
Back and forth
The wall
Finally sat down
And grew old.

662.

She pulled back
Her legs
The way one
Folds back
A sheet.

663.

The line
Wishing
To count
Its own dots
Turned around
In circles.

664.

He embraced
Life
At such a pace
That it
Let him go.

665.

When the bomb
Wanted to make
Room outside
It exploded.

666.

The fly
On the window
Asked itself
Where were the
Outside of things
And the inside of things.

667.

Roads are
Long hearses
Where the ground
Supports the earth.

668.

The shopping basket
Said to the eggs:
"Don't weigh
So much
Your shells alone
Are already
Breaking my bones."

669.

He kept
His thoughts
Unimaginative
So as to raise
The gravity
Of his ideas.

670.

The incongruity
Of her breasts
Is what gave them
Their charm.

671.

To regain
Its appetite
To amuse itself
The pig
Put itself
In a tin.

672.

She dressed
Like a whore
But was
Pure in heart.

673.

The pruned tree
Walked
In his jacket
In the town square.

674.

The water
Wanting to slim
Evaporated.

675.

The light
Shining thro'
Yellow flowers
Became
Its piggy bank.

676.

Shadow
Walked
With tiny steps
So that it wasn't
Broken up
By the stones
On the road.

677.

In the golden
Gladiolus
Yellow
Had
A hare-lip.

678.

Green
Was shedding tears
On the grass
And the sun
Drank them up.

679.

Her buttocks
Went so well
With her hat
That her dress
Flew up
Into her eyes.

680.

The sea
Listened to itself
Speak
And its sound
Became
Shellfish.

681.

The boulder
Tumbling in space
Gave out a shout.
It was its pre-echo.

682.

On the balcony
Of its breath
The nose created
A canopy.

683.

Overtaken
By tiredness
The bird
Flew
On its colours.

684.

The light
Became
Dull
Because of
The banners.

685.

She lost
The braces
Of her mouth
In a kiss.

686.

The water
Pissed
Among
The gorse
Which forced him
To open his trouser flies.

687.

The light
In the miser's eyes
Sold
At the going rate.

688.

The long grass
Tired out
The breeze
Which
Then
Went
To bathe
In the water.

689.

The soap
After being
Washed
Realised
It was dirtier
Than before.

690.

The trumpet
Cut its rope
And left
A large navel
On the water.

691.

The light
Projected
Fingernail shapes
Upon the onyx
And the flint.

692.

The bark
Said to the stem:
"Don't climb
Too far
You're pulling
My gloves off."

693.

Grey
Scrubbed itself
And became white.

694.

She lived
In the hollow
Of her breasts
In order to make
Room for men.

695.

When the egg
Saw the omelette
It had
A scrambled
Stomach.

696.

Only when she
Began to love him
Did he recognise
His own scent.

697.

The eye
Of the dying man
Contorted.
He could see
The interior
Of all objects.

698.

The dahlia
Had bad breath.
It had inhaled
Too much smoke.

699.

The sound
Of the horn
Escaped.
The car chased
After it.

700.

The dishes
Devoured
The eyes
And the man
Was no longer hungry.

701.

The eye
Bumped into
The stare
And fainted.

702.

The stench
Held its nose
The man
Walked on by.

703.

So afraid
Was the
Pretty little trinket
Of being broken
That it
Kicked up a fuss
Each time
Anyone
Touched it.

704.

The dead man
Awoke
And said:
"I see only
Dead bodies
Around me
Where am I?"

705.

The wind
Dislocated
Its wrist
Whilst putting
Back
The armrest.

706.

Mauve squinted
Because of
The nearby
Pool.

707.

The air
Was sleeping
On the shoulder
Of evening.
The wind
Chased after it
And embraced
The night.

708.

The egg
Swallowed itself
While it was
Being laid.

709.

Sweetness
Rightfully married
With acidity
Was cuckolded
By the salt.

710.

Light
Was running
At full speed
As night
Chased after it.

711.

Each stone
That fell
Into the water
Changed the light
Into a bracelet.

712.

The wind
Having lost its belt
Substituted it with a creeper.

713.

The mountain
Tired of climbing
Rested on the
High plateaux.

714.

The sun
Had
Freckles.

715.

This evening
The moon
Practised
Ogino.

716.

A rendezvous
Followed
The first time
Their eyes
Met.

717.

The moon
Purged itself
In the pockets
Of shade.

718.

Due to an absence
Of trees
On the plain
Shade left
On foot.

719.

At the beginning
Of Spring
Snow
Took
A Turkish bath.

720.

The plant's hair
Was messed up
By the wind's
Hair-raising
Breeze.

721.

Dust
Tapped a steady beat
To force
The wind
To make headway.

722.

Air
Made the
Snow
Waltz
To warm
It up.

723.

Decay
Consumed itself
And no one
Wanted it.

724.

The avenue
Of trees
Walked
Along the plain.
When it reached
The road
It began
To run.

725.

This evening
The moon
Slept
Using
The cloud cover
As a sheet.

726.

The hair-raising
Breeze
Was re-styled
By the grasses.

727.

The air
Fanned itself
With the sail.

728.

The mirror
In the habit
Of lying
Confessed.

729.

The bird
Striking
Against
The mirror
Believed someone
Had cut it
In two.

730.

The sea
Had filled up
To such an extent
That even
The wave drowned.

731.

The light
Went
To the cinema
And took its place
On the screen.

732.

The night
Took the moon
As a sleeping pill.

733.

The slope
Resulted
In the trees
Gliding
Into flight.

734.

The babbling water
Learned
How to communicate
With its source.

735.

Without permission
The water
Travelled
Through the town
After the rain.

736.

Lazarus
Raised from the dead
For the second time
Asked:
"Where's my coffin?"
It was in the sun.

737.

When
The female saints
Saw paradise
They ran away.
Because
There were only
Saints there.

738.

Everything
At midday
Loses weight
In the shade.

739.

She married
And after
The nuptials
Her buttocks
Resembled
The full moon.

740.

The sewer
Threw up
Continually.
And in this way
It advanced.

741.

She anchored
Her bottom under
The gaze of the man
And steered it into port.

742.

Diogenes
Extinguished
His lantern.
As he was
In the sun.

743.

The earth
Went for a walk
Without heels
Because of
The potholes.

744.

The walls walked
Stealthily
So as not to
Awaken the road.

745.

The pearl necklace
Around one's neck
Serves as dentifrice
For the skin.

746.

The reserved
Eye
Received
By appointment.

747.

The impure
Ointment
Came out in
Spots.

748.

Whiskey
Drank a soda.
Its throat was on fire.

749.

The haunch
Used light
As a skating rink.

750.

The car never
Caught up with
The speed
Of the road.

751.

The foliage
Of his nimble
Fingers
Pleated
The light.

752.

The water
Was overcome
By the final wave.

753.

The dancer
Was transfixed.
The room
Danced on.

754.

The rain
Blew its nose
For the duration
Of its last tears.

755.

It is
Only water
That kisses
Water
On the mouth.

NOTES AND ACKNOWLEDGEMENTS

Translating this book has certainly been a labour of love. These insights and ways of viewing life have infiltrated into my consciousness over the past four years or so since I embarked upon this task. But now I have finished and I feel a certain sense of loss. For without Monsieur de Chazal being part of my everyday life I fear that the colours may be slightly dimer, the flowers less beautiful, and the tropical birds may disappear altogether. And consciousness, the playful teasing consciousness of the universe, could gradually fade away until, regretfully, its very existence could be brought completely into doubt.

    And then again no! Now I consider these thoughts I realise that what is much more likely is that once one has dipped into the Chazalian mindscape one will always be affected by this at times colourful, insightful, surrealistic and humoristic way of seeing the life and existence within things. For to read de Chazal is to, among other things, appreciate that everything is made up of the same elements. And in some respects one can see an overlap between de Chazal's Weltanschauung and, say, native Americans' view of nature and the universe; animism, or as de Chazal puts it himself: *La vie derrière les choses.*

------ • • • ------

This book was translated to varying degrees in Majorca, Portugal, Wales and France between 2011 and 2015.

My unreserved gratitude goes to:

Fondation Malcolm de Chazal, and Yvelaine Armstrong – both for the initial proposal and invitation to translate Monsieur de Chazal's oeuvre, and the subsequent authorisation. Their respective help and encouragement throughout the course of this project has been very much appreciated.

Morfydd Bonnin – who proofread, checked, re-checked, discussed, considered, and helped translate many of these 755 aphorisms.

Finn Anson – for his wonderful help at the end of this project, for his insightful considerations concerning the text, his checking and re-checking and for the discerning suggestions and recommendations he made. His help has been invaluable. Thank you.

My thanks also goes to Sabri Karoui and Anne-Paule Mousnier.

------• • •------

On translation:

The three-way tug-of-war has been between maintaining the original meaning of the text, taking into account the rhythm of the words and how they fit together musically, and the maintenance of some degree of beauty and poetry that gets as close as possible to the sensation one experiences from reading the script in its original version. The nature of translation necessarily consists of decisions as to what sacrifices one should make and in which areas they should be made, to, in the final translation, arrive at the best approximation to the original as far as the individual translator sees it.

Here are a couple of examples of the quandaries experienced while translating Sens Magique.

313.

The white horses
Gallop up
The sea's foam
Beneath their hooves.

* *Moutons de la mer* in English is 'white horses'.
Hence literally translated this poem would be:

The sheep
Of the sea
Beat
Their own wool.

But here Malcolm de Chazal is using wordplay that we cannot easily translate since white horses do not have wool.
Another possible translation could be:

The white horses
Of the sea
Tan
Their
Own hides.

Another example is where, in one of the aphorisms, *mettre en boîte* is used. This means – to put in a box or tin. However, *mettre en boîte*, is also an expression that means – to mock, for example. Hence, the translator's job here is ideally to find an equivalent that encapsulates the two senses. If, however, this is not possible the translator must, nevertheless, convey the sense and feel of the piece as closely as is possible by other means…

Inevitably another translator would arrive at different decisions. I do, however, feel that I have conveyed the sense and the feel of the seven hundred and fifty five aphorisms as I see them and read them; that both respects and remains true to the originals.

Jean Bonnin
Pembrokeshire
Wales, UK.
November 2015

V1

www.redeggpublishing.com

www.ingramcontent.com/pod-product-compliance
Lightning Source LLC
Chambersburg PA
CBHW071156160426
43196CB00011B/2098